How to Confuse the Idiots in Your Life

Learn how to:
Baffle Clueless Questioners
Entertain Your Friends
Enjoy Your Very Own Idiots

by Ben Goode

Illustrated by
David Mecham

The Truth About Life ™

Published by:
Apricot Press
Box 98
Nephi, Utah
84648

books@apricotpress.com
www.apricotpress.com

Copyright 1999 by E. W. Allred
Sixth Edition.
All rights reserved. No part of this book may be reproduced
or transmitted in any form or by any means (electronic or
mechanical, including photocopy, recording, or any
information retrieval system) without the written
permission of the publisher.

ISBN 1-885027-10-9

Cover Design & Layout by David Mecham
Printed in the United States of America

This book is dedicated to all of those thousands of people who helped proofread this manuscript in a feeble effort to save me embarrassment... but only the ones who weren't reading it in its rough form just to keep from having to fork over a couple of bucks to buy the book after it was published.

A 'Sort-of' Introduction

There are few things in this world as satisfying as making a fool out of a fool. Confusing idiots ranks right up there with pro football, video games, and uncovering congressional scandal as a favorite American pastime. That's why this book is so important. We have spent a virtual lifetime* researching creative ways to respond to the questions posed by real and virtual idiots.**   You, our lucky readers, are the beneficiaries of this exhaustive research.

To begin with, we have searched the world over spending no expense to bring you thousands of years of wise responses, sarcastic comebacks, and subtle, rude answers to stupid questions. We have been able to accumulate dozens and dozens of profound sayings that look like they have come from all over the world and throughout nearly all of history, but that we mostly just made up. Even the legitimate quotes are usually from times and places that are so far off the beaten path that verification of their source is nearly impossible. Many of these responses are so deep that most emotionally stable people*** have no idea what is being said.

*A virtual lifetime is a cyber-lifetime and is nothing at all like a real lifetime

**Virtual idiots can be every bit as annoying as real ones.

***Probably you and me are about the only ones left.

When you interact with an idiot using one of our patented methods or one of our wise sayings, exciting things could happen. First, because our responses are so profound, some little teensy intelligence fragments may rub off and get on the idiot you are talking to, thereby making them just a little bit smarter and less obnoxious. In any case, they will certainly shut up and stop annoying you with their stupid questions for a while because they will be flabbergasted, stupefied, and unable to respond. And of course, anyone with half a brain who is within earshot and paying attention will enjoy watching the stupid, confused looks on the faces of your idiots.

Next time you are forced to interface with a bona fide idiot and answer one of his or her questions, pause, get a faraway look in your eye, and try one of the methods outlined in this book...

Contents

How to confuse the idiots in your life

A wise man once said, "Hey! what are you punks doing to my car?" While this probing question had nothing whatsoever to do with confusing idiots, it nevertheless was a good one for him to ask at the time. As we all know, there are many good, legitimate questions that can be asked in life. Unfortunately, YOU will never hear any of them. Since you are pretty much surrounded by idiots, your life is filled with stupid questions of the worst kind.

One of the great tragedies is that no one cares. I know I don't. In fact, if you think someone cares that you are surrounded by annoying idiots, take a poll sometime. Ask everyone around you whether or not they care that idiots are driving you up a wall. But let's not get side tracked. The important thing is that I have discovered a little bit of entertainment value in causing a puzzled, confused look to come onto the face of an idiot. So we are going to work on finding ways to help you get some enjoyment out of your very own idiots. This book is dedicated to achieving that goal. I have written down just a few ways to do this which might work. Go ahead and try some. We won't laugh at you. Honest.

A FEW WAYS TO CONFUSE THE IDIOTS IN YOUR LIFE

- When you make your phone message on your recorder, don't leave any instructions about what to do after the "beep".

- Tell a joke, leave out the punch line and then laugh hysterically.

- Tell a joke and leave in the punch line.

- Put helium gas in her asthma inhaler.

- Fry his tropical fish in cornflake

batter and then put them back into his fish tank.

- Change the aisle/floor configuration at the local Walmart Store.

- During the three-and-a-half hours that he's waiting for his computer to connect with the internet, have his screen-saver show a recording of the president's most recent grand jury testimony with calliope background music.

- Switch the hot and cold knobs on his shower.

- Drive the speed limit.

- While waiting in construction, have the pilot car leave never to return.

- While waiting in construction, have the pilot car leave to go 4-wheeling.

- Make the idiot have to follow the same laws that he makes for his constituents.

- Substitute an electric razor for her computer mouse.

- Steal all of his duct tape.

- Move your lips but don't have any sound come out of your mouth.

- Replace the brake pedal in his pickup with a whoopy cushion.

- Have all the rap, reggae, and rock radio stations play country songs and Rush Limbaugh.

- Print "Not to be taken orally" on her Captain Crunch box.

- Turn the batteries around in his TV remote.

- Have the "push" and "pull" door signs printed in Swahili.

- Just leave the "push" and "pull" door signs like they are.

- Have one of the extraordinarily busy corporate web sites re-route their customer complaints to her E-Mail

4

address. (This happened to me once and it definitely works.)

- Let her observe you cutting the tags off from your mattresses.

- Sew his fly shut.

- Configure the endless line of orange construction barrels into the shape of a maze with no way out....Wait, they're doing that already.

- Package beer in those annoying, little ketchup packages they give you at fast food restaurants.

- Hide his clean clothes on hangers in his closet.

- Cheer the good guys and boo the creeps.

- Shave her cat.

- Replace rest room stall locks with child-proof safety lids.

- Put her underwear in her sock drawer.

■ **Instead of gang symbols or disgusting graffiti, write calculus or trigonometry equations on bridge abutments and bathroom stalls.**

■ **Drive everywhere you go in reverse.**

■ **On a day other than Halloween, come to work in a "Big Bird" costume.**

■ **Make him use A.O.L. to access the internet.**

■ **Tape a picture of a vampire onto her mirror.**

■ **When he buys a home-gym, substitute the nutritional information for "Bake and Groove" microwave dinners for the assembly instructions. Wait...they do this already.**

■ **Replace his sun screen with analgesic.**

■ **Put the word, "NOT" in front of "Smoking Can Be Hazardous To Your Health" warnings on cigarette packages.**

6

- Change the dotted lines down the middle of the road so that they head off from the road and down through the middle of the golf course.

- Cut four inches off from his toothbrush handle.

- Fill his Crunch Berries box with Grape Nuts mixed with brightly-colored marbles.

- Move all of the brothels and bimbos out of Washington DC and into the Midwest.

- Make all politicians and bureaucrats work a regular job one month out of every year.

Profound, perplexing and entertaining come-backs to questions posed by idiots

After desperately grasping for straws for a few seconds trying to come up with a rational sounding "part two" for our book, we said to ourselves, "What the heck. Why not make up a bunch of bogus wise sayings that readers can use whenever an idiot asks them a stupid question that will leave the questioner so confused that he will grunt and walk away and the sane spectators will laugh hysterically?" To that end, we give you 6,000 years of deep thoughts from out-of-the-way times and places.

**Enjoy the beautiful sounds
Made by the creatures in the pond
While you can
Because soon the frogs may croak**

> •*Translation of an Ancient 7th
> Century Bonsai Haiku*

No one will notice that your fly's open if you walk into the room with your kilt tucked into your underwear.

> •*Medieval Scottish Proverb*

Whenever you get tired of viewing the lead-dog's backside, you can always close your eyes and visualize a cheese-burger.

> •*Alaskan Eskimo Maxim*

It's usually pointless to shoot your arrow at a buffalo that is already falling off a cliff.

> •*Ancient Native Canadian Saying*

It's better to aim your spear at the moon and hit only a rock than to toss your pipe bomb at a cat and hit your uncle Mel's Winnebago

> •*Palestinian Terrorist Youth Cheer*

Kitty litter is good, dude... but not for food.

> •*Egyptian Court Eunuch Training Slogan*

It's difficult to yell for help with foot in mouth.

> •*Mongolian Truism*

This sucks.

> •*A survey of the deepest thoughts of 10,000 American adolescents as interpreted by EKG machine.*

You suck.

> •*The winning piece of literature from a 13th Century London Teen Poetry Magazine, Modern English Translation*

They suck.

> •*A Popular 17th Century Young Russian Peasant Fable*

He sucks.

> •*Ancient Celtic Adolescent Side-Splitting Joke*

Everybody sucks so I think I'll go get my brain pierced, have a satanic symbol tattooed onto my spleen and listen to bad music.

•20th Century Adolescents Union Monthly Magazine Advice Column

A frost-covered outhouse seat yields few splinters.

•From the humor section of a 19th century Sears-Roebuck Catalogue

It's hard to swim with the fishes when your fins are chained to a concrete barrel.

•Sicilian Axiom

You will never gain the respect of the elder loan officers if you insist on showing up for your loan interview dressed in your sisters duck costume.

•From the Swiss Bankers' Creed

If you're gonna be a turd, go lay in the yard.

•Excellent Counsel from a Cro Magnon Psychotherapist

Beware the floating garlic cheese.

•North American Canadian Trout
Proverb

As you drift through the capillaries of life, may all the killer T cells you encounter be fooled into believing that you're only harmless mitochondria.

•Believed to be the greeting on
Hippocrates' front door

May the wind blow gently at your back and may the sun shine warmly on your face...assuming you're using a good sun screen, otherwise you could die from skin cancer.

•Ancient Hopi Indian Saying
(Hypochondriac's version)

Whenever your dentist gets out the chain saw, spit out the cotton and run for cover.

•From an Old Slavic Advice Column

May you always have success in your quest to irritate those you despise.

•Riga Mortis Vega

**Beware the monk
Who's traveled far
With whom you share
Your bread and cheese
If he needs a cloak
Don't lend him thine
When I did that
I got his fleas**

•Ancient Gregorian Chant

People who trim their toenails with large tractor attachments often have beat up toes.

*•From the Hottentot Farmers'
Almanac, Circa 1855*

Don't bother to blame the foul smell on someone else if you're the only one in the room.

•Good Logic

If the eyes are bugging out, the noose is probably plenty tight.

*•From the Olde West
Sheriff's Creed*

Whenever anything bad happens, find the guy with lots of money and sue him.

> •*Ancient Ethiopian Lawyers' Admonition*

By the time the Winnebago is parked on your head, it's too late to buy aspirin.

> •*From The German Tourism Weekly*

Whenever anything good happens, find the guy with lots of money and sue him.

> •*Belgian Lawyers' Saying*

If nothing much is happening, go find some guy with lots of money and sue him.

> •*Part of the Ancient Aztec Lawyers' Bar Exam*

If you haven't succeeded in getting rich by suing people with money, forget the law and go into politics.

> •*Ancient Etruscan Legal Maxim*

Whenever the mongoose has had trouble catching cobras and the eagle cannot see the rabbit, who cares; go find some guy with lots of money and sue him.

> •*From the Ancient Hindu Lawyers' Guide Book*

You suck.

> •*Translation from a Ming Dynasty Cantonese Adolescents' Poetry Book*

Never let your travel agent talk you into sleeping on a medieval torture rack.

> •*Transylvanian Travel Tip*

As you slide down the water slide of life, may none of your swimming suits give you a permanent wedgie.

> •*Ancient Polynesian Greeting*

When you wake up to the sun shining through mossy water, either you have been turned into a fish or something strange has happened.

> •*From "A Druid's Words To Live By"*

If the feller you're fighting has a big dog, be extra careful or you could get licked twice.

•Kentucky Coon Dog Club Motto

Never get into a cab driven by a crash test dummy.

•Part of the Detroit State Motto

It's tough to get kisses from a beautiful woman if you have a Kleenex stuffed up your nose.

•From the 1877 Issue of Hypochondriacs' Weakly

A few more ambiguous, sarcastic, rude, and evasive responses that appear wise, lack substance, and apply to most any stupid question.

Even small undies can give you a big wedgie.

•Little-known writings of Socrates

When you need a spatula to scrape Fifi off the pavement, it's probably too late to take her to the vet.

•Parisian Veterinary Truism

If the truck is parked on your chest, maybe you should spit out your gum as a safety precaution.

•Colombian E.M.T. Training Manual

Never go into battle with your underwear on the outside of your helmet.

•Roman Infantryman's Code of Conduct

Weeds and stickers in your socks are more pleasant than a poke in the eye with a sharp stick.

•I made this up

If the teacher has no DNA testing apparatus, you're probably safe blaming the booger you wiped on her computer screen on someone else.

•American Defense Lawyers' Ethics Training Book for Children

You suck.

> •*From the Lithuanian Adolescent Book of Wisdom*

When it's raining so hard that in order to breathe you need a scuba tank, the weather's probably too nasty to fish.

> •*Tahitian Mariner's Creed*

Never bet real money on a skinny Sumo wrestler.

> •*From "the Little Book of Big Samurai Wisdom"*

As you symbolically float through the arteries of life, may you never be assigned to convey nutrients to some sick person's colon.

> •*Medieval Swedish Surgeon's Greeting*

Never seek for urinals in a pink water closet.

> •*From a Book of Confucian Unpublished Random Thoughts*

When Hell has frozen over, it's too late for the devil to pay his gas bill.

•Puritan Thought Book

Fighting fire with fire doesn't mean putting out a person's cigarette with a torch.

•Mildred Disraeli

As you fly through the skies of life, may you never accidentally stick your face into a slightly used barf bag.

•Greeting on the outside of a bag of peanuts from the original Wright brothers' airplane

Whenever your brakes fail, it's okay to hit a moose.

•Alaskan Inuit Adage

A really cool belly flop can hurt body parts far away from the impact.

•Just popped into my head

Whenever it starts raining cats
and dogs, better go hide the mice and
cover the fire hydrants.

•*From an Etiquette Guide Book of
the Lower Amazon Delta*

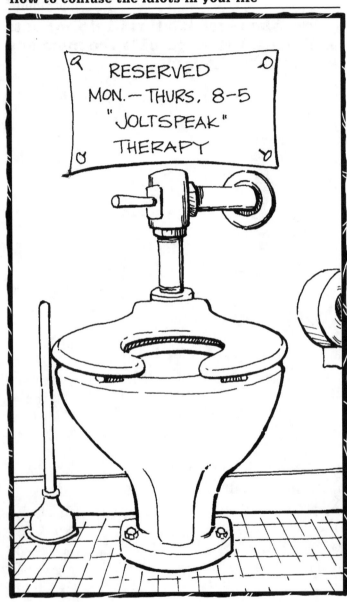

The art of answering stupid questions

Over the years, many people have asked me millions and billions of stupid questions. Over and over again I have been forced to answer such imbecilic queries as: "Why do you drive that piece of junk you call a pickup?" or, "Why do you leave your Christmas lights up all year?" or, "Did you know that your shirt doesn't match your pants?"

It used to be that on principle I would refuse to respond to such stupid questions. I was also afraid that stupidity was contagious and that if I interacted with these idiots, I might catch it. However, since I have recently declared myself the foremost expert on the subject, and, therefore, need to appear together and "with it" if I'm going to be able to get people to pay for my expertise, I intuitively understand that not only are these people annoying, but they are also stupid, probably complete morons. But still, even though I'm secure in this knowledge, people continue to ask me stupid questions. I hate stupid questions. With a passion.

Since I am a stupid-questions expert, and while I sit around waiting for the type of crisis to erupt which requires an expert like myself to run around and answer questions on all the cable TV news shows for millions of dollars per show, I figured I might as well write a book on the subject and entertain those of you who have so much spare time on your hands that if it weren't for the fact that you are reading my book, you would probably just be out holding up convenience stores.

Besides, there are some secrets that I have learned over the years that have allowed me to respond to stupid questions without shooting anyone-in fact, usually without even picking up large objects and clobbering these dorks over the head. Since many of my readers would like to develop this kind of composure, I figure I ought to share some of my secrets with them and make millions of dollars holding seminars. This requires the writing of a book. Of course, in order to have a book, one must have a secret to reveal. Since this isn't a particularly well-researched book and since most of what I am writing is pretty much just a bunch of hooey, I'm going to get my secret out of the way early so we can concentrate on peripheral, inconsequential, but entertaining stuff.

My secret bit of knowledge

The secret to responding properly to stupid questions is communication. Cool, huh? I can do this. Imagine for a moment that you are trying to communicate with a brick, a dirt clod, an ant hill, an animal rights activist, or a politician. Let's say you need to communicate with this brain-dead paper weight in order to pass along important bits of information. Let's say you would like to tell him that a group of ruthless terrorists with loaded, automatic weapons has been shaking down all of his friends and relatives, trying to get someone to tell them where he is...or that a dozen or so deadly poisonous scorpions just landed on his head and are crawling down his neck into his shirt...or that if he doesn't shut off the gas valve, his house is about to blow.

While he may feel absolutely no sense of urgency upon receiving this information, since he is an idiot, being the responsible party that you are, you nonetheless want to pass these facts along to assuage your conscience and limit your personal liability. In cases like this when you MUST communicate, I have used the following technique:

Technique #1 - Body Language...sort of

Communicating is more than just the words you speak. When speaking to someone with the brains of a barnacle, you must use every tool at your disposal. Many have tried with some success a technique I just made up and called "Jolt Speak." An example may help me share this concept with you: Let's say that you want to talk to your dense brother in law. Applying the "Jolt Speak" technique, the first thing you do is bend down and put your mouth right next to his ear, cup your hands around your mouth, and while looking very stern and serious, signal for your friends to begin lowering his head into the commode. Then, each time as they lift him out again, you deliver a brief part of your message. Use very small words and short sentences. Volume is critical. You should shout things like: "Next time" ...splash... "Before you have the crane drop the rocks" ...splash... "be sure the cab" ...splash... "of my pickup" ...splash... "isn't underneath." or "Next time you lock" ...splash... "the doors" ...splash... "make sure someone" ...splash... "has the key." Shout these short phrases in between dips. (In the event a commode is not handy, you can substitute a bucket of soapy water or Tabasco sauce.)

A word of caution is probably in order here.

Word of caution:

You probably shouldn't expect this technique to work. When I say that I've used this technique, I don't mean to imply that it ever actually did any good. You're dealing with an idiot.

If you want results, you'll probably have to come up with something better than this. Consider another alternative.

Technique #2 - A more subtle method known as "Sarcasmetrics":

Time and time again, when dealing with stupid questions, you will realize that in spite of everything you do, trying to communicate with blockheads is pretty much just a waste of good sound waves. However, since intelligent people might be watching, some kind of response is warranted. Here's an alternative: Forget trying to communicate wit the idiot. It's hopeless. Instead, use this opportunity to entertain the non-idiots in the crowd and maybe even impress them with your wit....The problem arises when we discover that you have no wit...or maybe you're just saving your very limited wit for a more important occasion. In this case, we recommend that you use the canned sarcastic come-backs printed in this book, or some like them. We call this technique "Sarcasmetrics" because we just made it up and think it sounds cool.

Try repeating some of the phrases that follow and let's see what happens. Since we have never tried this before, if you do use these phrases as recommended, let us know what happens... assuming that what happens is good. Otherwise, forget you ever heard of us.

A blob of sample sarcasmetric responses for you to practice on people you despise

Let's say that you're just minding your own business and some total dweeb sidles up and asks you a really stupid question like -

"Did you do your hair like that on purpose?"

A typical person of average intelligence might respond -

"Maybe I like it this way. You got a problem with that?"

As anyone can see, unless the wise guy responding is a whiny little twerp and, by offending some bigger guy might get beat to a pulp, this response has absolutely no entertainment value whatsoever. People watching will probably not be impressed or entertained.

Why not use a much more insulting and sarcastic canned response which you have memorized from this book, which, in addition to being entertaining, will also seriously confuse most idiots? Say something like -

"It's been a little hard to manage ever since I was hit by lightning." or "This is a disguise. I've gone under cover to try to catch evil terrorists bent on destroying mankind by disseminating chemical and bacterial weapons. I've found that I can get closer to them if I look like a victim."

See how much fun this can be? With practice, even you can learn to do this. Here, let's try a few more while you're learning to get the hang of it.

Imagine, just for fun, that you're on a long trip and some chowder head asks you a real classic idiotic question like -

"How much farther?"

In an irritated tone of voice, a normal person might respond -

"If you ask me that question one more time on this trip we're going to turn right around and go home."

As you can see, this type of an answer has

no entertainment value whatever and clearly stinks. Since you have to respond anyway, why not offer a response that at least has some entertainment value? A much better "sarcasmetrics" answer would be -

"If you ask that question one more time on this trip, you whiny, little twerp, I'm going to staple your quivering little lips to your pathetic forehead, stuff broccoli up your nose, and dump your suffocating body into the nearest septic pumping facility."

Or -

"If you ask me that question one more time on this trip, I'm going to tell all your wormy little friends that you wear Care Bears underwear, you stay up late listening to your Spice Girls CD collection, and that your mom and dad voted for both Richard Nixon and Bill Clinton."

See how much fun this can be? Here are a few more examples for you to memorize: Whenever some total goober asks a question like-

"Do you really plan to eat that stuff?"

Give the rational people who are within earshot a guffaw or two. Respond by saying -

"Hey Einstein, if you don't like it, you don't have to stick your face in between my bowl and spoon and watch."

Or -

"No, Bacteria Brain, it's a suppository."

Or even -

"You must be kidding. This isn't food; it's grout. I wouldn't eat it if I had just inhaled three tanks of nitrous oxide."

Some really stupid questions like the following require more thought. For example -

"Why does it seem that construction workers are never actually working?"

might be logically and sarcasmetrically answered as follows:

"Construction workers have a very difficult job. Because of the risks, there are certain weather conditions under which it is not considered safe for them to do actual work. These include:

A. A fierce blizzard defined as anything in excess of two snowflakes or rain drops within any 24 hour period.

B. A tornado has been sighted (anywhere in the U.S.).

C. Severe thunder storms, for instance, the kind that could come from those clouds over there.

D. Dangerous heat (over 68°).

E. Dangerous cold (below 68°).

F. A severe and life-threatening hunting season.

G. Major holidays including Halloween, St. Valentine's Day, Grandparents' day, Secretaries' Day, Boss' Day, Groundhog Day, Pets' Day, Bacteria Week, and The Annual Rutabaga Festival.

I recommend that while you are learning the sarcasmetric technique, you memorize these for occasions when you get hit with one of these classic stupid questions. And then you can save your brain for the more important stuff.

What kinds of people ask stupid questions?

There are those who would argue that there are really no stupid questions only stupid people...or something like that. To those who feel this way we would respond, "Hey, I'll bet you never had dealings with anyone in the White House or met any of the O.J. Simpson jurors." The truth is, however, that a scholarly work on the subject of stupid questions would not be complete without a bunch of trumped up, bogus, irrelevant studies on just what kinds of people ask stupid questions. Since we don't have any studies or solid trivial data, we are left with this: We have decided to lump all of the stupid questioners in the world into one of these three categories: Kids, Presidential Pollsters, and Dorks (AKA geeks, imbeciles, Cretans, losers, idiots, etc...).

Kids

Kids are constantly hitting you with impossible questions, most of which even they would realize are really stupid if they would just take a moment to think about them. They ask you about insects, food, the air, why your fly is open, puberty, why hippos don't fly, and a million other things that are so stupid that a rational person like yourself is completely unequipped to come up with the answers. Ironically, this can make YOU feel stupid and cause stress. Fortunately, youth is a condition that is usually not terminal and should eventually pass...unless you've fathered Gilligan, Dick Clark, or Dennis Rodman, or unless your kids also have an additional handicap, like they grow up to be a philosopher and begin to ponder questions like: "What's the meaning of our existence? What existence? Are there any absolutes? What came first, the chicken or the egg?

Pondering things like this is the third most unhealthy thing you can do right there on the list with sleeping on railroad tracks and actually answering these kinds of questions, which lead to conclusions like "I think, therefore I am", and "You can't teach an old dog new tricks."

If you ever find yourself hanging out with people who think like this, very quickly, before you have a chance to register to run for Congress, you must immediately check yourself into a treatment facility where you are forced to live on a ranch or in a subdivision or trailer park and work construction or wait tables for a year or so. This will straighten out your thinking.

Presidential Pollsters

Have you ever felt like you were being manipulated by evil, sinister people? Have you ever been asked questions in which you felt sure you were being set up, where the questioner was working to extract a specific response so that it could be twisted a half turn and used against you later on. If you have felt like this, you are either dealing with the IRS, or else you are undoubtedly one of the 11 people who are the exclusive source where presidential polls get their data. If this is the case, you must know that your responses are intended to manipulate the ignorant masses into feeling unpatriotic, or immoral, like there is something wrong with them if they sincerely don't agree with the majority, as represented in the polls. If you feel this way and if you are ever accidentally asked a stupid question by one of these pollsters, you have only one choice: Lie. This will give the pollsters something to do other than try to manipulate the rest of us.

Dorks, idiots, dweebes, losers, etc...

Respond with one of the comebacks previously outlined in this book.

Some questions & their answers

Knowing more than we really want to about many of our readers, we felt that this book would not be complete without additional responses to some commonly asked questions. To that end, we give you:

Relevant questions that I am often asked... and their correct and proper, albeit sarcastic responses

Question:

Dear Ben:

I HATE stupid questions. I hate people who ASK stupid questions. I hate people who ASSOCIATE with people who ask stupid questions. I hate the RELATIVES of people who ask stupid questions. I even hate people who only mildly dislike people who ask stupid questions. I find that I want to take all of the idiots who ask stupid questions and put dynamite into their ears so I can blow a hole into their barnacle-encrusted heads to see if there's anything in there. Is this normal?

Answer:

Yes.

Question:

Dear Answer Man, Ben:

I keep backing over my cats in the drive way. Fluffy was the third cat this week I've had to replace. I love my cats. Is there something I'm doing wrong?

Answer:

You might try putting the cats' little bed and their food some place besides right behind your car tires. However, before you decide to make radical changes like this to your lifestyle, you might consider this: Many scientists would argue that it's not such a bad idea to recycle your cats like you've been doing. This can improve genetic diversity in the local cat herd, plus the used cats can help you grow good lilacs.

Question:

Why do normally pretty stupid people become politicians and then turn into complete imbeciles?

Answer:

This is an age old question that I can best answer if I paint a scenario for you.

A scenario for you:

To certain types of sociopaths, power can be intoxicating. Picture some dork that nobody likes who, in order to validate his existence in his own mind, decides to run for political office. Since people who have brains, class, or principles generally don't want to spend most of their waking hours groveling for money while pretending to be something they aren't, while playing both sides against the middle and changing their fundamental principles and values every time the political wind shifts, normal, real people don't run. And so this loser/wannabe power broker finds himself running for office against some other principle bankrupt loser even slimier than himself. The voters are, therefore, left with a rotten choice, but since this slime ball happens, in this one instance to be the lesser of two evils...sort of, he wins by 2% of the 20% who, either out of patriotic duty, or because they are afraid they might lose some entitlements, fought off their nausea long enough to go down and vote. And their only choice was the lesser of these two creeps.

Now, this victorious politician, because he always believed his mother when she said that someday people would appreciate his talents, he, naturally interprets this great victory to be a mandate for his neurotic ideas and sleazy lifestyle. His frenzied mind concludes that the people have spoken and given him an overwhelming mandate to do whatever he wants and that all women lust for him.

Since he become a lawyer years ago, just so he could sue to get even with all of the people in the majority who used to beat him up because he was a spineless, obnoxious twerp, he now had the power in his slimy little hands, along with a fundamental understanding of the law, necessary to manipulate the world to his advantage.

In summary, he didn't just become a spineless, slimy low-life cur when he got elected. His election to office has just given him a vehicle to show his incompetence and lack of integrity. Is this all clear?

Question:

Dear Ben,

Why have so many government agencies and businesses gone to those time-wasting, obnoxious, frustrating, ridiculous automated voice answering systems?

Answer:

Simple. They have done this because it saves them millions of dollars. It saves them so much money because they can hire fewer employees because, thanks to their automated answering system, they have lost half of their customers and, therefore, sell only half as much merchandise. They can then spend the money that they saved exploring innovative ways to find new customers to replace the angry ones that they lost...except for the government, which doesn't care.

Question:

Dear Wise Guy,

Why is it that whenever I connect with one of those above-named annoying answering systems, I have to listen to the entire 2 hour recording at least twice before I can believe that there is no way for me to ever connect to the party I need to talk to?

Answer:

Why are you causing trouble? Why can't you just accept the fact that the party you need to talk to doesn't want to talk to you?

Question:

Dear Ben, the answer guy,

Why is it that after listening to a total of 3 hours of automated voice answering machine recordings and punching 37 buttons, that the evil machine finally puts me through to a human being and then at this point the actual person always puts me on hold?

Answer:

I don't know. However, you may be interested to hear of a new system that's being pioneered in corrupt 3rd world countries, which I hear is rapidly gaining popularity in this country called the "Celebrity System." After you reach the point where you are on hold, you punch in your credit card number. The automated answering system then ranks all calls currently on hold in order of credit card cash balances available. When you get to the point that your credit card balance is the highest still on hold, they take your money and you get your turn to talk.

Question:

Dear wise guy,

I love to eat animals. But now I have begun to feel terribly guilty. (Actually, I have no remorse whatever because I love to eat animals, my remorse comes from the fact that I feel no remorse about this and can no longer consider myself trendy and cool because so many people around me are trying to make me feel guilty because I eat meat and like it.) What can I do?

Answer:

This is a obviously a very complex issue. You are obviously a very complex person and, therefore, obviously deserve a complex answer. This whole problem is a function of the suppressed feelings of confusion that you have because these arrogant, holier-than-thou, vegetarian friends of yours have a prohibition only on killing "cute" animals which, in your logical mind defies logic. Remember, even professional animal rights people have no qualms about killing ugly animals like rats, roaches and bacteria and, of course, human babies, which will just grow up to consume some of the earth's resources. The key to good mental health is for you to decide which animals you want to think are cute and which you want to designate as ugly. This should be a matter of personal conscience. You can't allow your friends to make you feel guilty because you like to kill different animals than they do.

46

A few more questions, these about health, and a bunch of bogus answers

Dear Answer Person:

Whenever I jog or cycle, I get all exhilarated and then I become so excited to be out in nature that I unconsciously move my arms too fast, which causes friction with the air and my own dried skin molecules. Before I know it, my armpits have burst into flames. I'm worried that one of these times fire could spread to the hair on my legs and I could be permanently disfigured or lose all my senses and say the "M" word or something even worse. What can I do?

Gwendolan (Gwen) Granola

Answer:

You may have noticed that in this country, some ladies don't have big blobs of hair under their arms and on their legs. While I realize that many guys from Europe, who have loaned their brains to Jr. High science teachers for the kids to dissect, or who have had their brains damaged by falling earth-moving equipment (the same ones who get turned on by nose rings and pierced eyebrows and brains) find this body hair attractive on women. But many don't. It's conceivable that you could solve your problem by removing some or all of that hair and then you could stop worrying about arm pit friction.

There are two easy ways that you could do this: First, you can use pliers or vice grips and gently pluck it out one follicle at a time, or second, you might consider putting duct tape over the hairs and then giving a firm tug, removing it all at once. This will usually get it out by the roots so it will never grow back. And you won't have to worry about the risk of fire any more.

Question:

The hair that used to be on top of my head is gone. I've noticed that some other men also have this problem. What causes this? What can I do about it?

Answer:

As you age, everything on your body gets tired and begins to shift around. Your chest shifts down and becomes part of your belly, your belly fat shifts up creating attractive fat blobs under your eyes and chin. Because you are now expected to be responsible and work to pay for everything in the country, even your politics shift from support of drug-crazed, irresponsible, self-indulgent liberalism to narrow-minded, judgmental conservatism. It should, therefore, come as no surprise when you find that the hair on your head has shifted too. Tired of lying there on your head, it goes underground and later resurfaces in your nose or ears. Some of it retreats from off your legs and pops up on your back. You will also notice that the hair from your arm pits vanishes only to reappear on your wife's face.

A noted scientist* has argued that the actual mass of your hair remains pretty much the same as you age; it simply shifts its location.

If you are an onion-head who is losing your self-esteem or who gets tired of everyone teasing you, here are some of your possibilities: Your first option is to go buy a trendy hair-piece or "rug" that looks like road kill...and wear that. While people will still tease you, you will at least have a choice about what they tease you about. On days that you don't want to be teased about being a chrome dome, you can wear your rug and people can tease you about that silly thing.

A second option is to have pretend doctors sew what seriously looks like arm pit or pubic hair apparently taken from someone trying to raise money who probably lives in Southern Europe or The White House, onto your scalp. The advantage of this technique is that you don't have to worry about your borrowed hair blowing off in the wind or when some real man gives you a swirlie in the office commode. Also, you can take pride in the fact that it looks as though some pretend doctor stitched arm pit hair onto your head in interesting patterns.

A third possibility is to treat the problem by drinking one of those new medicines that can make thick hair grow on windows or pavement. The only negative side-effects of this approach are that the stuff tastes like frog vomit, will get you suspended from most international sports competitions and that you will want to howl whenever the moon is full.

A final popular treatment that you can try if nothing else seems to work is to have the doctors remove your "tired", hairless skin from your head and replace it with a patch of "active," hair-growing skin from some other part of your body such as the tops of your feet, your forearms, your wife's chin or the bear skin rug in your front room.

*Curious George

Question:

I used cocaine for 15 years, sometimes smoking it, sometimes placing it under my false tooth, but usually snorting it up my nose. I now have a very large hole in my septum and I'm afraid that it might go to my brain and kill me. What should I do?

Answer:

To keep your brain warm in the winter, have your mom knit you a little nose-warmer, or if your mom doesn't knit or if she is fed up with you, you can pick one up at a 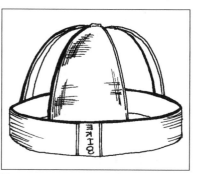 sporting goods store. You can even get them with a fly in front. To be double sure your brains don't leak out, try plugging that hole in your septum with the thigh bone of a cow or something.

Question:

I'm 11 years old and my mom says I'm impudent. I've watched enough C-Span and Geraldo commercials about the Monica Lewinski Scandal to know what the word means and now I'm worried. I'm too young for this. I still have my whole life ahead of me. Should I start taking Niagara, or Midol or some other drug now to head off the problems? Will the doctor tell my mom? If the Republicans keep control of Congress will they still be able to give us condominiums in 5th grade and will we still have school lunch and social security?

Answer:

Whoa , slow down little feller. Let's take these one at a time.

No.

Most likely.

That depends upon how the polls are worded.

Question:

What is a sure-fire way to lose weight?

Answer:

Caffeine Fasting. This is how it works: Begin a daily regimen of 2 Pepsis, 4-Cokes, 8-cups of coffee, 5-Mountain Dews, 4-Dr. Peppers, and a Nestle's Crunch. If you get hungry between snacks just grab a Surge or Hershey Bar. You can accelerate the weight-losing process if you only have a few days to lose some weight by supplementing one or more of the above drinks with diet pills.

A side benefit of going on this diet will be increased energy. You will get more done than ever before since fatigue will disappear, even at night.

The only known side effects are nightmares of swirling asteroid storms, heart attacks and shortened life expectancy.

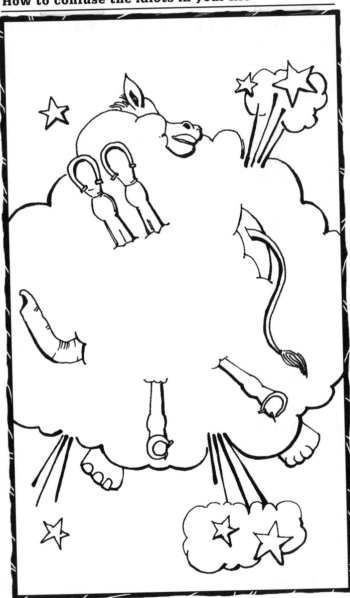

 # More health related questions answered

Question:

How do you tell if your psychic is a phony?

Answer:

There are many ways, but the best way to be certain is to perform the following test: Wrap a lizard up completely in duct tape. Next, fill a bottle with formaldehyde, put the lizard in and close the lid. Immediately call the psychic hot line and talk for 35 minutes. After you're finished, take the lizard out, (the duct tape should be pretty much burned off by the formaldehyde.) If the lizard cusses at you in Swahili while impersonating Elvis, and if the psychic offers to pay you $50,000.00 just because you're a good person with a lizard in formaldehyde, she could be legit. Otherwise, save your money.

Question:

My friend and I decided that we wanted to get our eyebrows pierced. Since we had no money, we decided to do it ourselves. Once we got started, we were afraid that my dog, Sparky, would feel left out if we didn't pierce his ears while we were at it. He was giving us that little sad dogie, "I want my ears pierced" look. You know the one.

Anyway, at the last instant, apparently Sparky got nervous and flinched. Is there anything wrong with going through life with a hot knitting needle poking through your leg? Are there any career skills that would be enhanced by this? Have you ever wanted to personally neuter one of your pets?

Answer:

No.

Yes.

56

Absolutely, I recommend it. It enhances bonding.

Question:

What is the difference between a Democrat and a Republican?
(Memo to idiots: This is not a health question.)

Answer:

A **Democrat** believes she has a right to force you to live the way she wants you to because only people supported in some way by the government are capable of compassion and understanding and because of a persistent feeling of moral superiority, which she feels because she never discriminates by reason of race, (only against white males and because of religion and political ideology).

Although she's promiscuous and a heavy burden on society because she's on the dole and even though she has had many abortions, she still has very high self-esteem because she recycles her pop cans and because she once went on a march to save the guppies and has a "Celebrate Diversity" bumper sticker on her YUGO.

Democrats believe that aside from

themselves, people aren't capable of managing the really important phases of their lives without government help, because everyone is some type of victim. They believe that it's okay if someone breaks the law as long as he is their candidate, that all military personnel are evil.

A **Republican** believes he has a right to make you live the way he wants to because he has a feeling of moral superiority, because he never discriminates against anyone because of religion, (only because of gender or race and socioeconomic opportunities). He believes a person is above the law as long as he supports free market economics and his candidates. He also realizes that all wars are good because we all get rich, provided we're not too dead.

Although he's pretty much a hypocrite, the fact that he holds higher standards for others, especially Democrats, than he does for himself does not bother him. He still has high self-esteem because he donated $100.00 last year to his alma mater's athletic scholarship fund and because he smiled and gave a noogie to a street person last Christmas.

Republicans believe that anyone who

isn't rich must be lazy. In fact, if they themselves hadn't had to wrestle with the burden of having been born rich, they would undoubtedly be even more wealthy and successful.

The last of the stupid questions and answers

Question:

Why does everyone out here hate people from California?

Answer:

There are reasons too numerous to mention, but here are a few:

Reason 1

Whenever Californians decide that the quality of life in the city is so bad that even fully Californicated people can't stand it any more, (This often happens after someone in the family has been shot in a drive-by shooting for the third or fourth time in a week while sneaking out to get the newspaper) they search to find a peaceful, safe, little town with none of the misery and squalor they just left. A few of them inevitably fall hopelessly in love with YOUR little town, which for good reason, has none of the terrible problems they are fleeing. Then they relocate their delinquent kids, who hate their new home town precisely because it has none of the misery and squalor, (not to mention danger) they are used to, and who take every opportunity to express their contempt for this picturesque backwater you call home.

As soon as they are settled in, they become militant activists who set about to change everything about your town to create of the danger, misery and squalor and to make it exactly like the place they just left, all the time whining about the way everything is done in your town.

Reason 2

Californians produce TV shows and movies written and directed to entertain their peers, who just happen to be self-absorbed, depraved, demented and dangerous scum and foist these upon the rest of the country.

Reason 3

They assume an air of superiority because their sports teams win everything because with that vast, urban economy and population base they are able to generate enough money to buy most of the talented players in any sport you please. These then set about transforming themselves from respected sports figures into bad actors, annoying rap singers, and drug addicts.

Reason 4

They think everyone wants to be like them. To help in what they perceive will be a difficult transition because we rural people are all such hicks, in every conversation they enthusiastically describe in great detail how much better things are in California, leaving us to ponder what it could have been that induced them to leave and why they don't return quickly.

Reason 5

They have eternally perfect weather (except for San Francisco which God placed in the middle of the state out of a sense of fairness) which would be okay except that in January, they have the audacity to call and ask about your weather and describe theirs over the phone.

Reason 6

Every so often, Californians do social research that is so advanced and brilliant that only they can understand it, like the research that culminated a 25 year study which concluded that children who are regularly beaten senseless are more likely to grow up and commit crimes which include beating other people senseless than are children who grow up with two parents raising baby kittens and who get daily hugs.

Then, based on these studies, they write up trendy legislation that is so brilliant that just like these studies, only Californians can understand it, like the kind that lets a guy go free who just finished cutting two people's throats because he had a troubled childhood and because some police who used to be racist now use tobacco in public. They do this to send a message to punish religious people, who they assume are out planning to blow up abortion offices, and to send a signal to the rest of the country that second hand tobacco smoke absolutely won't be tolerated.

Reason 7

Many people would like to have their lives considered relevant. Because the media and movies, which are all produced in California, naturally have such a fascination with California's demented pop-culture, and THEY decide what should be considered relevant. These lords of the trendy proclaim that firemen, construction workers, school teachers, clerks, parents, fat people, old people, adults who act like adults, God fearing moral people etc... are of no consequence.

Everyone except for the indolent rich, Hollywood types and young, beautiful people are tired of having Californians symbolically shout at them that their lives don't matter and they need to drink more beer.

Reason 8

(Write your reasons here:)_____

_____

_____

_____

_____

_____

_____

_____

_____

_____

_____

_____

_____

Question:

Why is it that I have never ever met or even heard of any one who was ever polled in a national made-for-TV poll?

Answer:

Because the people you associate with think like you do and the polling people don't want to hear your opinions. They don't want word to get out that anyone thinks like you do. It might harm their agenda.

Question:

Why are young people today so stupid, so wimpy and weak?

Answer:

When we oldsters were younger, back in the good old days, people didn't have as many soft, easy things. Take for example CDs. When I was a kid, most of us were so poor that we had to make our CDs out of tin can lids, or even whittle them from wood. That's why we thought some of the best sounds were made by Barry Manilow, Bob Dylan, or Johnny Cash. Me and my buddy, Bryce, even made our own cell phones out of two tin cans connected with a string. Today's young people complain about dead spots and poor reception. Heck, we had to keep the string tight and could only call people within shouting distance.

Question:

I just became a vegetarian because of intense social pressure. After two weeks of this lunacy I have discovered that I hate eating weeds and pulp. And the anger is building up inside of me to the point that I would sincerely consider eating the people who put me up to this. I sense that these feelings are not trendy at all. What can I do?

Answer:

Most doctors, psychotherapists, and out-of-it rural people recommend prime rib.

A Brief Chapter of Unrelated Material to Take Up Space, Some of Which is Pretty Stupid

"Nobody in football should be called a genius. A genius is a guy like Norman Einstein."

NFL Broadcaster, Joe Theismann

I just got lost in thought. It was unfamiliar territory.

Bumper Sticker

He who laughs last thinks slowest.

Bumper Sticker

See a penny,
Pick it up
And all the day
You'll worry about catching Ebola,
Flesh-eating virus, or something
worse.

American Neurotical Society

Remember, love is not heart-shaped. It's circular. That's why it's so difficult to distinguish between a well-rounded person and a big fat zero.

Rich Hall

"Smoking kills. If you're killed, you've lost a very important part of your life."

Actress, Brooke Shields on why she should become a spokesperson for a federal anti-smoking campaign

When the chips are down, the buffalo is empty.

Montana Bumper Sticker

People who chronically break the speed limit are acting out their intolerance of authority, namely law

enforcement officers.   And that's good!
If you enjoy speeding, try getting a
personalized license plate with the word
"VOID" on it.   That way, when you get a
speeding ticket, the officer will have to
write "VOID" on the ticket.

Rich Hall

**See a penny,
Pick it up
And rap music will make you
Want to up-chuck**

*Professional Rodeo Cowboys
Association*

**"They brought me up with the
Brooklyn Dodgers, which at the time
was in Brooklyn."**

Casey Stengel, 1962

**See a penny,
Pick it up
And all the day
You'll have a penny**

Hugo Greenspan

"If the people don't want to come out to the park, nobody's gonna stop them."

Yogi Berra II

"I failed to make the chess team, because of my height."

Woody Allen

We used to say, "Good riddance!" Now we say, "Let's have lunch sometime."

Alex Ayres

A veteran golfer was constantly defeated by the 13th hole. That hole always got the bette of him, always made him finish up one or two strokes over par. He told his wife, "when I die, I want to go back on that 13th hole if it kills me! Promise me you'll have my ashes scattered all over that...13th hole." And sure enough, when he died, after the funeral, his wife solemnly scattered his ashes all over the fairway-and the wind blew them out of bounds.

Bob Monkhouse

One day a derelict approached Mark Twain on the street in Hartford and asked him for a handout. Mark Twain sympathized with the unfortunate fellow and offered to buy him a drink. The tramp said he didn't drink.

"How about a cigar?" suggested Mark Twain.

"Sir, I'm hungry," said the tramp, 'but I don't smoke."

"How would you like me to place a couple of dollars for you tomorrow on a sure-winner horse?" Mark Twain proposed.

"Sir, I may not be the most righteous man, but I never gamble," said the beggar, somewhat haughtily. "Please, can't you spare a quarter for something to eat?"

"I'll stake you to a whole dinner if you let me introduce you to Mrs. Clemens," said Twain. "I want to show her what becomes of a man who doesn't smoke, drink, or gamble."

The technique of giving convoluted answers

I know that this is supposed to be a book on how to answer stupid questions. But, I'm afraid it wouldn't be complete without some tips on answering questions that aren't obnoxious and stupid. There are times when through no fault of your own, you get caught doing something you shouldn't and someone like your parole officer, spouse, banker, or special prosecutor is required by law to ask you some not so stupid questions, which, if you answer them truthfully, would get you into big trouble. For many of you, it could be useful to develop the life skill of giving what the experts call "convoluted answers."

One of the best ways of doing this is to answer a question with a question.

Example Question #1:

"Did you set fire to your own house?"

Your convoluted answer, (another question):

"Why is it that the only way you can ever be sure to get an important phone call returned is to go sit in the bathroom?"

Example Question #2:

"Did you have relations with that woman?"

Your convoluted answer:

"Have you ever wondered how different the echo system would be if butterflies had big teeth?"

Example Question #3:

"Didn't you realize that you had a stop sign there?"

Your convoluted answer (a):

"Isn't it much more important for us to work together in order to have peace and harmony in the world?"

Your convoluted answer (b):

If the "second question, convoluted answer" technique doesn't work, another often tried and well-proven type of convoluted answer is the attention diverter. The key here is to dodge the question all together while launching an attack on the questioner.

Example Question #4:

During your fraud trial, the prosecutor asks you a legitimate question like: "Were you aware that on your loan application you put down that your income was $47 million -a-year, when in fact, you are being kept by your parents who live in a trailer court on their social security and give you an allowance?"

Attention Diverter answer:

You might respond by suggesting that you have solid unsubstantiated rumors that the lawyer questioning you is a child molester with a methamphetamine lab in his basement. Or you could ask the jury how many of them have been guilty of parking illegally?

How to react when seemingly normal people ask stupid questions

There are times when you are caught off guard, when some seemingly normal person asks you a truly idiotic question. What can you do?

Not long ago I was hauled into court for my 4th speeding ticket of the year. When it was finally my turn, I walked to the front of the courtroom and witnessed an amazing thing. The judge, who, since he was a judge, we may presume had had decades of the finest schooling, kissed hundreds of backsides to get his job as a judge, and who should have been one of the most savvy, street-smart, together people in the world, called me up and asked me: "How do you plead?

Those of you who have spent a good portion of your lives in the slammer or who, for some other reason speak fluent legalese will immediately recognize this as a judges way of asking you, "Were you really speeding?", which I'm certain even a certified dolt would recognize as a VERY STUPID QUESTION. In fact, this falls into the "classic" stupid question category since all drivers know that the only time when normal, healthy people are NOT speeding is when their car is broken down, and since the officer clocked me at 82, there was obviously nothing wrong with mine.

I began to worry about the quality of our courts and law enforcement people until it dawned on me that he was probably just pulling my leg...so I went along with the joke and quipped, "Sure, my car was broke down or I would have been going 160." To which the judge fined me for contempt, suspended the jail sentence for the speeding part and probably went home to watch Judge Wappner.

The moral of this story, if it has one, is that unless you are a trained, professional stupid questions expert like myself, you probably shouldn't try to get in on law enforcement and judicial jokes. You probably shouldn't jokingly ask the baggage inspection people at the airport if they want to see your cool bomb. It might be a good idea not to pull your hands out of your pockets quickly while hollering "SURPRISE" after armed police men have shouted at you to freeze. And it's probably not a terrific idea to make jokes about your secret Swiss bank accounts during your IRS audits. In fact, you probably shouldn't joke around with any seemingly normal people who ask you stupid questions. Better yet, let's just forget this whole chapter on normal peoples' stupid questions and keep practicing responses for the idiots in your life.

 **More wise sayings that will confuse idiots and entertain friends**

I bet you wouldn't be feeling sorry for yourself today if you were dead.

> •*From a 19th Century Bavarian Beer Drinker's Motto*

An angry bee can never fly up the nose which already has a finger in it.

> •*Arab Truism*

A waist is a terrible thing to mind.

> •*Some guy being interviewed on T.V. said this*

You know you've been sleeping too long when you blow your nose and dust comes out.

> •*Ancient Transelvanian Saying*

In the middle of the night
When your deep and scary dreams
Have you floating in the ocean
Or swimming in a stream,
Don't let yourself get too relaxed
Yes, wake yourself a bit
Cause if you're smiling with relief
You'll wake and be all wet

> •*Mongolian Pre-Trance Warning Chant* -- (Very difficult to translate precisely into English)

May the witch doctor never try to cure your hiccoughs by pouring Tabasco into your loin cloth.

> •*Pre-Columbian Aztec Good Luck Wish*

A wise salesman doesn't waste time trying to sell bacon to his rabbi.

> •*Yiddish Proverb*

Once you can conquer your conscience, anything else is easy.

> •*Nero...endorsed by Ted Bundy, O.J. Simpson, Jack The Ripper, Johnny Cochran, Dennis Rodman, Richard Nixon, Bill Clinton, Geraldo Rivera and many others*

Before you jump off a cliff, test the parachute on someone you don't like.

> •*From a NAZI Paratrooper's Instruction Book*

As you symbolically flow through the veins of life, may you never be caught hanging out with a bunch of leukocytes who wind up discharged as blood in the stool.

> •*Ancient Greek Physician's' Greeting*

It's hard to soar with the eagles when, because of the turkey squirts, you can't leave the commode.

> •*Doorman Vincent Peel*

Look on the bright side, you're still out of prison because none of your close friends or business associates has been elected president.

> •*From the Law Code of Hammurabbi --*
> (imprecise translation)

A frog doesn't act so sassy after you drop him into a blender.

> •*From the Opera, "Of Mice and Middle School Shop Teachers"*

This Sucks.

> •*20th Century Adolescents' Words to Live By*

If the other ducks are made of wood, don't land on the lake.

> •*Good advice from the unpublished directors' cut of Downy Duck grows Up.*

You suck.

> •*From a book of 18th century North African Adolescent Thought*

Never give someone a piece of your mind without first stopping to consider whether or not you can get by on what's left.

> •*Wyoming Proverb* --
> (I didn't make this up)

You have some advantages that the rich and famous don't: You have to do something weird or perverted like running naked through city hall in order to get your picture in the newspaper... and your dog likes you.

> •*From the Philosophers of Monte Carlo*

The cheese never tastes quite as good after your head is smashed under the mouse trap wire.

> •*Turkish Rodents' Axiom*

So your personal life is a disaster, at least the earth hasn't been hit by a large meteor during this epoch.

> •*Standard Council From Neanderthal Psychotherapists' List of Snappy Come Backs*

Just because a person shoots a bunch of school kids, sells heroine to expectant mothers, takes a grandma hostage, steals everything of value from an orphanage and tortures a puppy doesn't make him or her a bad person.

•Trial Lawyers' Creed

If you plan to live in Warsaw, it's best to cool it with the Polish jokes.

•From a Calcified Prehistoric Slavish Fortune Cookie

Like surfing a tsunami, when you get feeling sorry for yourself, it's hard to stop suddenly.

•Taken From a Tahitian Gift Booklet

While a positive attitude won't always make things better, it will annoy enough people to be worthwhile.

•17th century Soroptimists Creed

If you are trying not to sneeze, don't poke grass up your nose.

•From the Mayan Warriors' Hand Book

May all the people who wish you ill wake up to find their tongues have been stapled to railroad ties.

> •*Ancient Hun Farewell Greeting*

Protesters don't shout so loud when their mouth is full of tank treads.

> •*Observation by Chinese Communist Party Leaders*

May your masseuse never become so confused that she puts itching powder in the lotion bottle.

> •*Athenian Good Luck Wish*

A broken nose is often a cure for allergies.

> •*Hypochondriacs' Manifesto*

Whenever the bill collector on your doorstep flashes chemical weapons, maybe you should consider paying up.

> •*Old Longshoremen's Axiom*

Men with back problems shouldn't lift pianos.

> •*Line from the Operetta, "Clementine"*

"A good case of colitis is a better weight-loss program than spending the night in the vomitorium."

> *•From The Big Book of Roman Humor Ca 71 A.D.*

"Don't feed the bores."

> *•Advice from the original "Travelers' Atlas" written by Marco Polo's Mongol brother-in-law, Earl*

"This just proves that you should never tie your dog up to a strange semi."

> *•Very good advice given by Timmy after giving up trying to find the first of what would eventually turn out to be eight Lassies*

"We've upped our standards. Up yours."

> *•Internal Revenue Service public relations advertising slogan*

"You shouldn't hide your over-the-limit trout inside your underwear."

> *•Sound fishermens' advice*

"The blind man may not properly enjoy the sunset. The deaf man probably won't sing along with the oldies on the radio. But the sleeping man will always say nonsensical, off-the-wall things whenever the phone rings in the middle of the night."

•*From the Pseudopigraphic Book of Bible Humor By Willard, The Monk Circa 1400 BC*

"Never take Fifi into China Town."

•*From The Big Book of Dogs' Wisdom*

About the Author

Born of mixed-racial parents, (His father was a Male, his mother, an ardent Female) Ben grew up during the Viet Nam era. Like most young men at the time, he dreamed of being a war hero. Unfortunately, Ben was rejected by the R.O.T.C. even though he had learned his times tables and he never wet the bed any more because he was only 9.

Finally, years later he achieved his military dreams by joining the war on poverty where, against tremendous odds, and in spite of great social pressure, he managed to avoid going on welfare. During the battle of Central Washington University, having been reduced to mere farm labor, heroically, he kept his young family from starving.

After a brief period of prosperity, against his wife's wishes, he decided to re-enlist and join the war on drugs. Here he distinguished himself by brilliantly avoiding all illegal substances. In fact, he would have been completely drug free except for sneaking an occasional antihistamine for bad allergies and a Pepsi.

His writing career was dealt a severe setback when, in 1995, against the advice of his wife and 2 teenage daughters, he wore white socks to a book signing at Barnes and Noble in Greely, Colorado.

This book is an attempt at a literary fashion come back.

'The Truth About Life' Humor Books

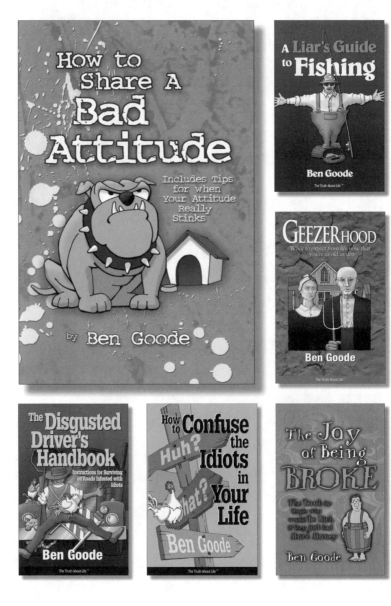

Order Online! www.apricotpress.com

Apricot Press Order Form

Book Title	Quantity	x	Cost / Book	=	Total

All Humor Books are $6.95 US.   **All Cook Books are $9.95 US.**

Do not send Cash. Mail check or money order to:
**Apricot Press   P.O. Box 98
Nephi, Utah   84648**
Telephone 435-623-1929
Allow 3 weeks for delivery.

**Quantity discounts available.
Call us for more information.**
9 a.m. - 5 p.m. MST

Sub Total =

Shipping = $2.00

Tax 8.5% =

Total Amount
Enclosed =

Shipping Address

Name:

Street:

City: State:

Zip Code:

Telephone:

Email: